EARNING YOUR FIRST MILLION

EARNING YOUR FIRST MILLION

Real Stories,
Practical Steps

CASSIDY SILVERWOOD

QuantumQuill Press

CONTENTS

Earning Your First Million: Real Stories, Practical Steps

INTRODUCTION

I have taken it upon myself, in the process of self-discovery and the lessons I have learned in the few years of taking the decision to seek financial freedom, to reach out to some successful young Nigerians in that regard and write about what I have learned. I categorized the book into six basic financial freedom steps. First, whom should you associate with? It's a well-accepted fact that interests of a person are a function of those who surround him or her. Second, learning about money; what have others used money for in the past. Third, which type of business should you invest in at the beginning when funds are not that much? Should it be active income or passive? Fourth, psychology of money. After focusing on the financial freedom steps, I looked at other practical steps - books about business, real estate. I ended with some practical business and investment opportunities available to the reader. I have introduced real money cases from over 20 individuals. Some examples were weaved into the necessary P.S.,

21 principles of business from Richard Branson, and 67 steps to achieve mastery in any business more from Amancio Ortega.

There have been several books on the subject of money and wealth building. Some focus on finance, some on investment, while others on the psychological side of money. But there are very few success stories from Nigeria that are documented and provide practical insights. It is said that the rich get richer and the poor get poorer. In light of that profound truth, it would be useful to learn firsthand from those who took the boldest steps needed to break out of the poverty cycle.

CHAPTER 2

Setting Financial Goals

To see that I could meltdown financially and that I needed to provide myself with safety. Three components: investments for health, time, and money. The first two, as many consider, should come first, but let's agree that nobody will invest or go in for one's health if one has a goal. The third one is a bit more controversial. However, considering that time passes mostly as a result of changes in our health - we inevitably grow old - to my mind, you will not miss while working out the three pillars of stability. It is important at this stage not to be greedy and allow yourself to articulate your goal - as specific and goal-oriented as possible without breaking the edge between reality and your capabilities. This is exactly what I did: I qualified working as a manager in a construction company, though I really got a practice as an economist in "Centerdorproekt" firm. Your task is to go on living without any shocks, which means choosing a possible way of achieving the goal.

One year before I started at the university, I realized what financial stability and independence give you: time to decide, responsibility for choices, health, and giving. I stopped trying to find the best price for jeans I admired, stopped looking for a way to save owing to coupons when going out with friends, and even decided I could not afford extra classes for better preparation for the examinations. We lived in the center of Donetsk in a nice apartment, went twice a year to the beach, and in style to school - thanks to my uncle, who paid for everything. But it was an approximate understanding that somebody else was paying for my life, and it was not right. I was going to be a doctor, and it was the way to financial independence, but no matter what, I pursued a license to give primary medical aid. Any simple emergency case could not undermine the financial stability of my family again.

CHAPTER 3

Building a Strong Mindset

The outlook of achievers like us is crucial when it comes to creating wealth. Also, government figures reveal that there are 80% more self-millionaires than wealthy lottery winners, a fact repeatedly stressed by the national entrepreneur magazine during the last couple of years. "There is a great deal of research that shows that if you have earned your first million once, then you are much more likely to earn it again together with even more money. This is due to so many contributing factors. For one, business people and entrepreneurs have contacts and a network that increases over time as they get to speak with more and more people," explains Anders. To many of us, he has become the personification of success, possessing an exciting ability to earn big sums of money. Throughout the years, Anders has bought property, stocks, and airplanes. He has also donated money to organizations such as the Hommerfonden and the Red Cross. How does he help increase the success rate with the new Trender subscription? "One key is that we have identified a group of successful entrepreneurs who guide our customers. These are just like Anders, that have amassed money once, but also people that have set up successful businesses with turnovers amounting to over US$ 2.5 million dollars and have a record of increasing profits year after year. They have had numerous companies and so know everything about starting up businesses."

CHAPTER 4

Developing a Solid Financial Plan

On one end is "I have 1,000 dollars but don't know where to buy a samogon", while on the other is an esque millionaire that uses the words: "consultation from the United States", "boats in Florida", "maximum grip load", "clip chip Texas" broke all the same antediluvian ferriate - the main thing is that it has not been used, they all go to the same place. (Blasting). Every successful businessman has started his business by selling something. Computer disks, sugared popcorn, carts, $ 2 cassettes, fake perfume or sanctions in the General's Dacha. And we all began with only one thing: nothing. Carsten Maschmeyer - the German billionaire, F.W.Dickins, lacking anything but cash, the first thing he began to sell - suits. If you have already built the basics of a solid foundation - accumulated initial capital that allows you to create a business on the long run, it makes little sense to invest all of your savings in stocks. This way of investing is for those looking for diversity to avoid part of the credit and simplify their lives, or are passive investors, putting some money in the portfolio every month.

Chris Morris: Pessimism should be unacceptable to you, while the most upbeat, pathologically optimistic person must always be aware that they could lose everything in one week. This implies that you must have insurance for everything, no matter what happens. This is what good financial planning is. What if I die? What if I lose my job? What will I do in the event of illness? What if I get sued? What if my house burns down? We, the people of Ukraine, have been too spoiled with expensive cars and the availability of loans. I have connections, I will always pay - this is one of the thoughts. And I am not an exception. Money for investing should never be borrowed from anyone. If you decide to let someone talk you into a process like this, in any case, never give anyone a property where your children will live over the years along with their parents.

CHAPTER 5

Managing Personal Finances

To save 1 million dollars is an immediately solvable problem. A professionally managed investment portfolio offers an average annual return of 10% nominal and 8% net of taxes and inflation. As of today, in the US, investment bonds yield 2% per annum. Corporate stock dividends offer an approximate yield of 4%. 30% taxes and 3% inflation result in an annual geometric mean of 8%. If you are afraid of subjectively perceived risks, invest in the US government bonds that have never defaulted. Theoretical risk is reduced to the real debt of the US government. If you are afraid for your children's future, invest in the rental of tract houses. In the US, they could be rented throughout the 20th century – through all crises, wars, and terrorist acts. Before you make your household investment decision, read "The Millionaire Next Door," a book by Thomas Stanley and William Danko. Any serious investor will tell you that you have to take calculated risks. If you want to increase the investment growth rate, do business rather than just invest received money.

Very few lucky people inherit wealth from family members. The rest of us have to work to achieve financial independence. In the modern world, life can be comfortable if you make one million dollars and deposit the money in a reliable bank. What to do if you want to earn one million dollars for your happy retirement? Yuri Musyatov, a financier, entrepreneur, and author of over 70 co-authored books, shares his experience. For people living in economically developed countries, this amount is not the top of an iceberg, of course. By Yuri Musyatov's definition, one million dollars is the necessary amount of start-up capital, sufficient to provide for oneself and one's relatives, have a rest when you want, and not to be afraid of something unpredictable.

CHAPTER 6

Investing Strategies

Whether you want to buy a house, fund your retirement, or maybe handle obligations related to family that are a couple of years ahead, the longer you're willing to let your money compound in stocks or in other investments like furniture and handicrafts, the more wealth you'd be able to create. The first concept to address when discussing the investment approach is asset allocation. It's what decides how much of your investment funds should be in stocks versus bonds, real estate investment trusts (REITs), commodities (e.g. gold or silver), fine wine, and collectibles. The aim is to create a balanced fundraising so that any negative performance in one category is softened by another. For example, while most stocks, especially small cap and technology stocks, showed double or triple-digit losses back in 2001, good government and corporate bonds experienced double-digit returns. This is how you manage risk and benefits of investment. The asset allocation within your investment can be seen as real estate investment in different parts of a large city.

Many would-be millionaires aren't because of their belief that you need a lot to invest, to invest consistently, or that the stock market isn't for you. Understand that even saving is investing. Saving is putting money aside for something in the future. Investing is the same thing. Saving is putting money aside for buying things or meeting your needs in the near future, while investing is putting money aside for the long term. Investing starts with saving. The two go hand in hand. It's difficult to invest without having taken the time to put something away to invest. It's also difficult to invest consistently without saving. You never reach financial bliss with the one-time joystick saving or investing. Consistent saving of relatively small amounts is what creates wealth. Have a separate fund or account for investing. It's the one that allows you to handle risk and work towards long-term goals. This isn't to say that investing just involves putting money in something you may not need in the short term, but rather the belief that the money can grow for a significant period of time and help you achieve important goals in the future. Any money aside from an emergency fund, or what you would need in the short term or to handle various obligations that are only months ahead, shouldn't live along with money for your long-term goals.

CHAPTER 7

Real Estate Investment

Firstly, if you are going to invest in real estate, contemplate residential properties. Acquiring and letting homes will unite you in a business structure that you can be comfortable with. Once you understand these options and have foresight on how matters are going to operate, investing specifically in residential properties takes on more faculty. You may not need to waste on renting real estate or real estate that will cost you a lot. Earning a bigger amount of possessions not only reduces the venture of missing them to vacancies but will also impart you revenue. You may also want to diversify and decide on apartments or homes—the least it calls the low-end linger area. This will also give you a perceptible hypothesis liable on someone going for a buy or a deal. Lodging costs gasped construct while real estate costs fall.

A property is generally a store of capital or some value of property. So, real estate investment means any investment in real estate which holds an interest for deeded interests, leasehold interests, further investments, access of interests in real estate, options, trading real estate, or advancing funds on behalf of real estate. Now, the question emerges: what are the factors that support real estate ventures? Although the general valuation is stable and the property is genuine in natural law, the goods and offers can be compromised and determined. Currency flow can also appear over time, as well as on an eventual sale that will support investment benefits.

CHAPTER 8

Starting a Successful Business

In the article, I presented a list of nine secrets of the world's most successful businessmen. Nevertheless, those entrepreneurs became successful because they knew they could rely on their keen instincts and skills to realize their ideas - ideas that had nothing to do with attending official business courses. The following article will help you find some potential businesses you can key into without attending expensive business courses. Some of the readers who have read this book have decided to become rice farmers, vegetable suppliers, Obioma gé Nkemis, and so on to ensure that their actualization of a profitable business can easily be enhanced.

There is no denying that every person has the talent to make money - but only the ones who genuinely search for real opportunities and positions that will help actualize that money can actually come up with successful business ideas. We have all seen, met or even heard about the local woman who inherited huge wealth from her deceased father, but ended up with nothing because of her inability to come up with a great business idea. Just think about that young man in your town who boldly went to the city with nothing in his pocket, but returned immediately as a millionaire! Thus, inventing opportunities that will make you very rich in the future does not mean you have to undergo academic courses.

CHAPTER 9

Building a Professional Network

Using the experiences, learning, supportive or just observing successful people is always exciting and useful. It is possible to make a huge income from the experiences and explanations of the people who have crossed the bottomless pits on the way you go. You are beyond the application, product, project, shareholding, management, internationalization, financing, acquisition, and operation principles of your own business. Maybe one of my resources is confusing or not valid for you. Then go over the others, you will find answers to your problems or questions in the light of different experiences. At least the options and solution patterns will be known and will provide convenience in the necessary points later. It is also possible to encounter best practices of all concepts as well as business areas, finance, investment, marketing, HR, sales, and development strategies. And at least you will see that you make mistakes when you are shown other alternatives and solutions. You immediately correct when you see the mistakes you make according to the person writing, the path you went and you will minimize the costs. Alternative approaches to doing business or developing your career will help you become successful.

Explained by experts as social capital, your professional network symbolizes the relationships you build with others. A professional network is built over the years of meeting people, communicating, and personalizing relationships. As I underlined several times, digitization is excellent, but do not minimize the importance of meeting people and creating relationships. The biggest collaborations and all opportunities come through the network you build. When you come to the right place in meeting people, you start to recognize people from sectoral organizations that I share within my resources. In Turkey, it is a small country as well as in the world. It's more efficient to watch a war you will win not under a tent, but in your own room by recognizing the players, not the nomination. If you are not happy with the business people around you, if you want to add new ones, I will end with one suggestion. You can get help from the network of people you respect to make your first meeting start faster, or you can meet someone in a pleasant way at a conference I am regularly participating. Otherwise, you can move to the USA, left to right, wherever you want. R&D is also necessary in relationships.

CHAPTER 10

Leveraging Technology for Financial Success

The standards and most of the tools for the financial decentralization of the economy were created within the first couple of decades of the World Wide Web. 25 years have passed since the time of their wide distribution and have not left indifferent technologies for stock trading, the issuance of financial information, the creation of thematic product sales platforms, thematic magazines, lifestyle stories about the investment success of the middle class, obtaining international qualifications in the field of trading, real, bonds, and options, as well as in various aspects of economics and finance. With their help, worthy people born in the New Economic Mechanism of the USSR almost without any state and foreign assistance successfully integrated into the modern international financial and economic system.

Modern technologies and the internet most fully reveal their capabilities when it comes to earning money. They open up many separate channels for making money to people all over the planet. At the same time, as talented financial analyst Brent Takoma notes in his book "Road Map: How the Rich Do Not Make Mistakes in Money", even millionaires are not too enthusiastic about various modern digital and internet technologies. Why? Because they do not appreciate the insufficient level of security of many of these technologies. However, this is no reason to ignore such opportunities as the real-time operation of a network of thousands of computers, huge reserves of knowledge and technology in the public domain, regardless of the complexity, and, most importantly, without intermediaries, taxes, and the eyes of official authorities. Not only did the entire crypto-economy appear.

CHAPTER 11

Overcoming Obstacles and Challenges

The more you go through such situations boldly, without losing sight of your vision, the stronger you become, the calmer your brain is and more insights come your way. With lots of patience and reliance on your faith, you overcome them one by one. The wisdom gained from handling these challenges successfully leaves you rejuvenated and ready to tackle other seemingly more complicated ones – without the slight need to stand back for too long and ponder. These challenges also give you the best opportunity to know what can work and what cannot work in any situation. They are the downs that greatly help you in appreciating the ups when they come your way. Understanding that experience is the hat that any victorious business person wears, when stung, one immediately shrinks back to prepare himself, return to the drawing board and to come back more forceful than before, this time around richer in terms of experience.

Never underestimate the power of a challenge because it brings out the best in you. It's also a great source of inspiration and motivation. It comes in many ways and forms including washouts, huge losses, severed business relationships, death of family members, ill health, fire to your business premises or stock, theft, interest rate hikes or even being taken to court or accused of not being totally honest with your client. At some point, you are your own biggest enemy. This is when some ex-friends wish you more challenges, not because you are close to failing but because they worry about your fast progress and they are not prepared to pay the price you have promised to pay. All these are the plain and simple facts. They are challenging, wearing, heartbreaking, draining and one is, at times, better off concentrating on the solutions rather than the cause.

CHAPTER 12

Maintaining Financial Discipline

The top two richest people in America have been consistently ranked as numbers one and two in list of incredibly successful people based on net worth since the 1980s. How do they get there and stay there? One dollar saved and invested may not seem like much. But over time, the miracle of compound interest allows America's wealthiest people to sit on net worth metrics that double or more every six years. It's not the dollars themselves. They own shares in assets that generate money. Of the 52 wealth-building strategies millionaires were asked to choose from to suggest to those still learning in business, nine out of ten put purchasing frequently owned dividend stocks in the top five of all the items listed. This proven pathway to wealthy lives is something that everyone can do and is one of the reasons many millionaires are back in the top net worth ranks two years after they've returned because they made perfect financial decisions that led them to ruin in the first place.

Millionaires have a wide range of things they do to maintain financial discipline. Here are ten tips that they shared. It's easier to save money if you don't spend very much. Doing so needs to become a deeply ingrained habit. Once you become used to the luxuries and conveniences that come with success, they are hard to give up. Stimson says that cell phones were a great example. A few bucks very month doesn't seem like very much. But he dumped AT&T for T-Mobile, saving $1,000 a year, discovered he never used that kind of data at all (using a 97 cent per day data only plan) and turned off sprint on dozens of other immaterial services. Together, a year of cost savings quickly became worth a $5,000 investment toward his long term saving goals. This isn't about cheating you. This is about making good choices on what really is expendable and where you truly get value.

CHAPTER 13

Achieving Financial Independence

But if setting wealth as a goal could be a great mistake and therefore it will be defined as "more" while you just need to think in terms of financial independence. In this regard, I personally prefer to measure wealth by two other indicators: wealth happiness ratio, for which happiness is identified as being rich in time, experiences, and interpersonal relationships. In the case of all these three kinds of wealth, you dream force yourself not to reason in terms of monthly or annual income, but rather to identify the capital necessary to guarantee you the absolute maximum security for yourself and your family. Once this capital is identified, you must go in pursuit to achieve financial independence, which will then be made known as the Soft Landing on Beach of Happiness.

You can set your own personal goals - these will be our compass in life. I have achieved my first million and it is a subject for pride, but it is not the most important thing in life. In fact, in order to achieve real financial independence, you need much more. In fact, you need to earn not one but at least seven million. Why? Because in a more lucky and thus more successful moment, at least seven million will be necessary as a lifeguard which will help you to live on this money and not work anymore, without diminishing your financial potential. Therefore, the real result of financial independence is the possibility to generate annual revenues from luck, from your property, from your deposits, etc. equal to at least 10% of your net assets. The easiest and most reliable, because guaranteed by the state, method to obtain this kind of financial independence is indeed always to invest in the government.

CHAPTER 14

Creating Multiple Streams of Income

Passive incomes are the least common income among the 177 individuals in our study. This is more normal among proficient or high-income individuals who understand finances. Passive revenue is also the only method to be financially independent. Becoming passive only happens after engaging in a saving plan for a long time. The main benefit of this income is that it will help you outlast an employment loss or business failure. The writer also gave room for explaining how to create passive revenue, it took financial discipline and also the ability to manage your finances. Six techniques are presented in the text to help readers succeed in practicing their active incomes and to permit the generation of passive incomes in the future.

Nearly all the millionaires in our study created multiple streams of income to build their fortune. Even if they had one day job, they could also have a side business, earned sponsorships because their name dropped heavily in the basketball court, or married someone who earned money and together they developed various businesses.

The reasons you want to start creating multiple streams of income are because, while one business or career is more protected from risk, the others could still have a lucrative market. And if you are to practice a good investment and savings plan, you are not required to put cash revenues back in your business and instead could investigate other investment alternatives. Being the weakest brand of the three, working towards creating multiple streams of passive income should make you less vulnerable to the downsides tied to relying on one source of revenue, like losing your job or going bankrupt because of your business.

CHAPTER 15

Maximizing Tax Efficiency

Let's assume that a $50,000 investment compounded at 5% grows to almost $435,000 over the next 40 years, and that the investor buys, sells, receives dividends, and makes swells once every five years. After paying an overall tax rate of 28%, his investment is worth almost $252,000 after taxes. Ouch! The investor's after-tax wealth is less than the $250,000 invested. But now let's consider how this investment would have fared if the investor had been tax-efficient. After 40 years, the investment would have grown to about $1.4 million, versus the $3 million he would have accumulated if he had been tax-inefficient. While tax-efficient investing avoids those painful tax bites, the likelihood of being tax-efficient declines the more actively the investor trades in and out of stocks, the more income he realizes, and the shorter the time he holds particular stocks. The same principles apply to contributions to tax-deferred retirement savings vehicles. With an annual earning rate of 5%, a $50,000 investment will grow to about $185,000 after withdrawing at an effective overall tax rate of 28%. But if the investor waits and derives income at a much lower 15% tax rate, after-tax wealth will balloon to about $570,000. Of course, 'tax deferral' represents the strategy of allowing an investment to grow, tax-free until it is liquidated.

When calculating the amount of pretax income you will need to pay in order to invest $100,000 per year, the obvious answer is $100,000. However, like an ice cube that melts away to nothing as the sun's rays hit it, income taxes can destroy your purchasing power, eating away at the money you have worked so hard to earn. And the same is true for taxes on short-term and long-term capital gains and durations. I advise investors to pay attention to tax efficiencies of their investments.

CHAPTER 16

Diversifying Investments

The hard part was creating a financial plan that was realistic, do-able, and profitable. We intended to make money when the market is bad; it is just as tricky to earn from a bull market but when we would be needed less. Newly acquainted with the intricacies of diversification, we wanted to save one year of our Year 1 (2017) take-home pay so now that we can be better market timers—an investment sought not just in knowledge.

The easy part was selling insurance, inviting many people to attend a Financial Planning seminar, courtesy of our colleagues in our now-in-house mutual fund provider, and meeting and talking to our venture-in philanthropy partner, ATRAM, for the seminars of all company entrants, Tita Le Lebumfacil for a life insurance company partnership, and for other money-earning (not necessarily income) capabilities.

Diversifying is critical for successful investing—something you need to do to beat high interest rates eroding your money. We knew we could never succeed in our quest to earn P1 million within one year without the expertise of an economist, an accountant, and a stock market analyst—what we may not know or possess and integrate yet. So we sought the CPP: our Tito in New York, our CPA-UP College of Business official and business consultancy, i.e. Eon Consulting, our economist pedagogue Sir Fernando Aldaba, and our stock market analyst, our future brother-in-law, Mark Sexton.

CHAPTER 17

Embracing Risk and Reward

Every time you undertake a project, an investment, or a hiring decision, the first question to ask is not whether you'll succeed or generate value. It's what kind of mistake can you afford? That's not a flippant question. Two kinds of mistakes will kill your fledgling business right away. The first is betting everything you have on one roll of the dice. The second is assuming that you'll get everything right from the get-go. To mitigate the first mistake, be absolute about your downside risk. I'm constantly amazed by the number of really smart people who take on business risks without considering their personal downside. You need to think and define this clearly—what would happen to you personally if a venture failed. Ask 'what's the worst-case scenario' and figure out how to survive—otherwise you are playing, as I put it, Russian Roulette with your personal and economic life. Instead, find ways to ritualize your fear of loss and prevent yourself from getting too carried away. Decide how much you can afford to lose. If the business or career decision goes sour— make sure you'll live to play, or invest, another day.

When you realize that you cannot prevent all mistakes, it becomes easier to cope with them. In fact, it becomes imperative to welcome that risk and then mitigate it. Turn mistakes into a source of knowledge. I'm not foolish enough to celebrate mistakes for their own sake —particularly mistakes that could have been avoided through better planning, or that produce unnecessary costs. Yet often, the prohibition on mistakes is so pervasive in the corporate world that people live in fear. Innovation, entrepreneurship, meaningful change—all require the willingness to act despite a lack reliable information. The framers of the U.S. Constitution understood that trial and error are inherent in the quest to create a more perfect union—there's room for them in your quest to advance your enterprise and your career.

CHAPTER 18

Scaling Up Your Business

What works without a push in competition, and even with a competitive field, may not be noticeable at all. Where do people's interests and skills lie? Second childhood was my question recently? I had examples of starting a kindergarten in a neighborhood, a sports nutrition store in front of a sports hall, and land plots around the cottage village, which were suddenly very popular. Service pies before it becomes a cleaning company, and one's daughter twig tied 30 thousand rubles in 4 weekends working as a childcare entertainer in a completely different city. They choose areas of development for themselves and spend money to increase their own welfare (food, rest, health, children's education, real estate, interest and hobbies, pets). Suburban real estate, especially in new buildings or in the built-in house areas, where schools, kindergartens are already built or the process of building is tied to millionaires.

How can you estimate how long it will take to earn your first million rubles by scaling your own business? In the beginning, you should be planning all your actions for the first six months, a year, two years, etc. Think up your image of a rich man and act in the image of a rich man now. Accumulate experience and knowledge:

only the rich can find various niches and introduce programs that will bring in a lot of money. Once, more than six years ago, I was told about all the richness of decisions, thousands of people, and barely controlling the situation, when a partner and I published a very serious letter about some problems (real and not really), with references to all references (about 60-70), and I received 2.5 million rubles in 4.5 months. Now let yourself have 10-50 such problems. Find growth areas.

CHAPTER 19

Identifying Lucrative Opportunities

Learn to pick. Some work is more promising in terms of income, "if fishing is a big fish, try not to break the network, and if you have good partners, don't go fishing." You can make your work less effective: "I have only five percent of my time doing business that brings 95 percent of the profits." What conclusions are interesting for business when developing your business, what can accurately reflect its strategic essence and priorities; and in every new business or activity, ask yourself how we will act in similar circumstances in order to spend as much money and time in the most efficient way. Ask yourself what we are supposed to do, identify your business strengths and make a decision based on strong business people.

Working more and more, we believe that we are moving to our cherished goal: to become richer. However, working at seven, there is another very important concept: "Learn to say no." "We could have obtained any of the businesses and the business we refused (Robert Gallston)," "Business says not only to what we do, but also to what we do not do."

CHAPTER 20

Mastering Negotiation Skills

There are a few basic principles that guide on how to become effective in negotiation. The major way of approaching negotiation is the interest-based method, where parties seek to look beyond their own desires and work together to find value-creating solutions that would be of benefit to both parties. Here let me digress a bit; one mistake that the average guy on the street always makes is to always seek to have the last percentage in any negotiation. Someone seeking to buy a house of 10 million wanting to pay 8 million, and those selling the house wanting to have 60% of the price, and ultimately the parties walk away without having their interests met. Any major deal can and is always done in human emotion, knowing also that two people might look at the same thing and see different things, but they must resolve to fight over the principle most of the time.

"It's not what you ask in life that determines the quality of your life, it's what you negotiate." ~Richard Shell. One of the most important skills that I have developed in my quest to earn my first million is the art of negotiation. I first came across the concept at the stock market when I bought my first shares; most successful traders had some secret formulas that they used as trading signals. My curiosity was awakened, and it made me very inquisitive. Most of the successful analysts I found out that the moment price reached a certain level, they swung into position. I wrote a few of the formulas and tested them, by and large, they were able to bring in profits. Big money is made in the smallest of details; you need to master the secrets that work.

CHAPTER 21

Balancing Work and Personal Life

I won a lot of money but I now have a new and unexpected relationship with money. I can spend it all now because I know I can make them again. I appreciate money like a 5-year-old that just got offered some pennies by his grandmother. I still dream of spending the night in a carousel under a rain of candy but I cannot picture anymore of how this fantasy activity could help me grow. I carry big plans and analyze hundreds of business opportunities every year. But what I want is quietness with my girlfriend; time to cook and share dinner with my family; to enjoy the deeply inspiring moments of the year; to travel through the beauty of this world. Assuming risks. This is the key concept that any successful entrepreneur knows upside down. You assume risk, you will work and plan to reduce the probability of failure knowing that the probability of success will go against market returns at the same time that would be impossible to achieve without this same increased probability of failure.

The most important statement I have to make is that I am a successful man. I have grown and developed as a person while creating a high net worth business that makes people happy. I am an educated person but I am not a super brain. I am a hard worker that uses his education to gain advantages. I have a happy personal and professional life that does not make me choose between them. I am a winner because I built a high net worth business that has shown resilience and capability to grow. Not by chance, not by co-incidence. I created an opportunity and took it. I assumed great risks and played a game with the cards that were given to me. I trusted no outcome and fought with my people, with my environment, with a past me that was weak.

CHAPTER 22

Planning for Retirement

Begin by saving effectively for retirement, the dividends, interest, capital gains and rents that you make as described in chapter 8 post-mid-life or during the retirement phase maybe sufficient to maintain your desired lifestyle provided that you did not overburden yourself with financial obligations during early stages of your life, and that you understand that drawing high amounts of capital from your business as dividends consistently instead of plowing most of the earnings back into the business, and occasionally taking out reasonable salaries from earnings for land or property development, depletes your business reserves in the form of retained earnings as well as cripples your business, because this is not allowing the business to run on surplus the way it should, given the benefits that you could have received by wealth creation through committed business surpluses that would have been employed expansively.

You may not be giving too much thought to retirement at this nascent stage in your career. When you think retirement, it seems so far into the future (and really, you are right; it is). You think you can always start planning in another few years. However, it is important to note that time is the ultimate factor one can exploit to achieve financial goals, and given that there are fewer goals in life that need to be achieved earlier than a comfortable retirement, then it suffices to note that it really is essential to begin financial planning for retirement early on in life. That said, I am also of the opinion that the returns from your personal business should also have been wasted potential if, from the strategy that you trained yourself to employ earlier on in life, those returns did not support you in retirement, given this potential that the returns had in you.

CHAPTER 23

Giving Back to Society

So, for me, giving back means earning my next million by enriching the lives of those who can't yet do it themselves. Sometimes people make the mistake of taking everything that life can give them, never asking themselves if it's worth the price. They may never find the answer to that question, for they have not lived the lives of those who have yet to ask it. When you share your experience and enable others in their pursuit of a better life, society benefits as a whole and you, in more than just a symbolic way, get advanced from the waiting line for the Nobel prize for Economics. In a broader perspective, we have to understand that each life improvement essentially betters life for all of us. For everything we do we affect our reality and prolong its existence, just as our reality is affected by everything created around us. That's perfectly okay so long as we realize that notions like goodness, kindness, compassion, and gratitude are no longer religious, old-fashioned, and outdated, but practical lessons of responsible behavior, without which we cannot begin to heal society and connect as a species in order to survive and prosper as individuals.

When everything becomes clear in business and you find yourself in a rewarding, fulfilling, and secure situation, that's the moment when you start searching for a way to express your gratitude to society for giving you a chance to earn your first million. You shouldn't take receiving from society for granted. True, it does demand a lot from you, even while constantly giving you opportunities, but it's worth the effort. By giving back, you not only do a good deed but also set an example for others to follow, and creating examples for others is something that can change the world.

CHAPTER 24

Learning from Successful Entrepreneurs

It is so for leaders who begin from a tabula rasa and proceed out into the wide world to check what is there. Regrettably, most of these leaders fall and fail to reach their dreams. This includes top managers, government representatives, startup founders, and all those who wish to become outstanding figures in their field. The world is too multifaceted, and each business is unique. It is no secret that the truth behind the immortal catchphrase "A leader finds his path where others merely see obstacles" is nothing other than a PR myth. So do not aspire to be a leader from the very beginning but rather start with striving to transform 1 percent of someone else's success story into your own experience. These first 1% will open a new path for you. They will be followed by valuable knowledge and skills in addition to a strengthened sense that success is possible.

After analyzing many entrepreneurs and their businesses, I have discovered a certain pattern. Twenty percent make a breakthrough on their own and successfully develop their business. But eighty percent of entrepreneurs learn from other successful entrepreneurs.

They got their first billion (or first million, for those first starting out) as a follower—and only then did they become leaders in their own business market niche. This eighty percent has spent from several months to a year and a half to achieve their first results. Why does it happen like that?

CHAPTER 25

Achieving Long-Term Wealth

25.2 Set large and small goals: This is the secret of the wealth of Roman Avdeev, an entrepreneur, investor, banker, philanthropist, and now State Duma Deputy. I have always been conscious in my goals: I do not seek to create another commercial project, and not even a network of business projects, but a real corporation with an innovator in every area. I don't stick to plans and concepts – I often change them. I weigh it long ago. If my life had gone differently, until one and a half years ago I would have been standing at some kind of State Bank, opening my mouth every 10-15 minutes and listening carefully, without interrupting the "normal" banker. And I don't even know what kind of person I would be right now. I have another goal – to illuminate and draw attention to the fact that it is possible to design and invest in great startups in a country like Russia. My "dream book" will be very humane. Because everyone will want to touch the beautiful and actually clear the windshield of their soul from mud. Some will succeed, but a much larger number will not.

25.1 When you're starting out, skepticism may be more useful than reinforced optimism: "The best teacher is failure, as it is failure that chastises and beats into the head," says Leonid Mikhelson, businessman, President of Novatek. You can only count on a healthy take-off when you feel the ceiling with your head. In the first six months of the start of Navigator, I visited almost all regional sales offices of the company. I had to return to the head office 3 or 4 o'clock in the morning by car after visiting a dozen regional offices, and at some point, the car turned in the opposite direction to the navigator, going in the right direction. I realized that it was necessary to change the whole concept of work from scratch. Without understanding and admitting my mistakes, I would hardly have achieved what I achieved.

CHAPTER 26

Staying Motivated on the Journey

2. "You have to have someone on your side with the same objectives." Girley Wright, 45, Metairie, La., divorced; managing broker, Abpco, a mortgage company. Net worth in 2001: -$25,000; in 2013: $1.3 million. Girley Wright never intended to be in the mortgage business, but she had a goal: buy a house by 30. "I worked on growing my credit and saving money for it." She began in the late '80s as a computer programmer doing home mortgage analysis for Alexis & Associates, a Bank One company. After 9/11, the economy took a nosedive, and Alexis eventually went under. Wright emerged with 29 default-and-delayed home loans, having advanced those funds to lock in rates when the storm hit. "I found that if I could take the best aspect of how the mortgage industry operated on a national level and combine that with smaller companies' occasional flexibility, I could turn it into a profitable business," says Wright. She now earns additional revenue and a pension from a prior 19-year career in software programming. But by the time she hit and passed her 30-year goal, she was far from done. "I jump into something, get it done,

and then need something else so I keep going," Girley says. Now it's getting through the downturn in housing.

1. "I try to limit where I go if it's unnecessary." Suellen Robinson, 43, Glendale, Ariz.; married, life and health insurance agent. Net worth in 2002: $1.1 million; in 2013: $1.1 million. "I try to limit where I go if it's unnecessary," says Suellen Robinson, a married, self-employed life and health insurance agent from Glendale, Ariz. Cutting costs was key for Suellen and her husband Steven, 48. "We set a goal to retire early and made sacrifices along the way." Cutting costs was key for Suellen and her husband Steven, 48. "We set a goal to retire early and made sacrifices along the way," said Suellen. "And if you're at Panera Bread and it's happy hour and you shouldn't get that sugar cookie, walk away." Echoes Steven, who has a background in finance and runs his wife's office. "We may not have the things other people do. But we're still incredibly content and happy."

Work hard, be patient, and stay on course, and money will come. These are the simple secrets three could-be financial posters are living by and sharing in becoming millionaires. Here are their sayings:

CHAPTER 27

Navigating Economic Cycles

- Rise. Because you don't do anything that will make you think less of yourself later. And because I don't think that you end up rich if you're not especially proud of your own activity. - Maintain. Because if you're already rich, you don't need to strut to be proud of your own activity, you'd do something bad to be ashamed of yourself later. - Act. Because you're not still rich. - Dive. Because now, when everyone's climbing, you shortlist the best of those who've fallen. From a range, through ratio-sized bites. - Graduating. Because savers want cheap assets, so now it's better to stay poor. But the times of distress also force decisions that will allow you to multiply earlier EUictos. It is then good if you are able to do it, because you do not greed when others are greedy (you cannot then earn hardly). You can look further, but there is no extreme gain on shares from a long-term peak for several years.

The role of economic cycles in personal finance management has been discussed in previous posts, so I won't repeat myself (see the topic list). Here, I'll just mention that the concept of economic cycles should be included in all discussions of personal finance man-agement. It's analogous to computer science reps learning universal principles of organizing programs, from algorithms to automated program development, before moving on to specifics of certain programming languages. Let me quickly offer five suggestions for managing your personal finances.

CHAPTER 28

Protecting Your Wealth

Despite the greatest achievements being necessary to make a legacy, and despite your focus on wealth protection, nothing is completely safe. There will always be people who will want to take your money. Acknowledge this threat as part of life, take measures to limit it, but also think about the deeper reason behind these attempts: people want to take your money because they need and want money. They need it for shelter, food, and fun; they want it because money always bodes opportunities, no matter how skeptical you've become. You've learned that money is a leading power tool. Enjoy it, but always with a clear mind and humble heart.

I cannot stress it enough: Lawsuits are part of success. Even if you do everything right, you can still be sued, often because of envy - telling people what you have is the worst thing you can do. If someone starts talking to you about stocks and asks how you did, it's foolish to open up. How you tell your friends, family, and acquaintances about your fortune is up to you, but remember that opening up can lead to trouble. The larger your wealth, the more people will start taking notice, and the more trouble you will have to fend off. As soon as that number reaches a certain level, people will start looking into how to harm and sue you. This goes for everyone who has ever achieved anything extraordinary. There will be inevitable attempts to poke holes in your success.

CHAPTER 29

Investing in Stocks and Bonds

So, if stocks have such an outstanding track record as a wealth-creator, why do so few of us choose to invest in them? Simple: stocks are riskier than just about every other asset class. If you invested $100 in stocks at the start of 1962, by the end of 2017, you would have grown your stake to $5,707. Not bad at all. But your $100 could have experienced some exceedingly tough times. In 1966, a few years after you'd invested, you'd have lost over a quarter of your money. 1969 was even worse; you'd have almost lost one-fifth of your wealth. Stock prices didn't start to recover until the late 70s, and it would be another decade before you felt really good about your investment. What slowed your wealth's come-up? Irrational exuberance, so says Alan Greenspan, and stagflation, notes Ben Bernanke. In other words, bad things that happen to economies and markets. It's not just the stock market that has a history of risky ups, downs, and all-arounds. While stocks are usually doomed to see-saw, most well-diversified investment accounts will too.

Recent surveys have found that over 70% of Americans view the stock market as the best place to invest over the long term. However, data indicates that only around half of all Americans actually own stocks, either directly or through mutual funds. For black households, the percentage falls to 24%. That's a shame because stocks have historically earned more money for investors than any other asset class. As an asset class, American stocks have appreciated – current market hiccups notwithstanding – by almost 10% per year over the past century. That's over 3% per year more than long-term government bonds, 5% better than Treasury bills, 5.5% more than cash, and nearly 7% more than bonds issued by large American companies. If you do not invest in stocks, you will be missing what has historically been the best wealth-generator on the planet.

CHAPTER 30

Building a Strong Financial Team

The best businesses are the ones that have been transferred by group leadership. Constantly join groups where people share the same entrepreneur profile as you and have knowledge on issues that may help you to level up with your companies. Exploit the experience of these people to improve the way you act, to think and to handle the situations you do not know well or are not prepared to act in. Experience is not transferred from jugs to third grade people. It acquires experience through contact with the present and future leaders in the field you want to learn. Networking helps us to reduce the learning curve. Don't shy away from inviting successful people from other areas to provide business lectures. Promote business seminars, network and dialogue on the subject. Only we present the biggest members with the opportunity to establish businesses after deep surveys. We must exploit the experience of these people to improve the way we act, we think, and to deal with the problems that we do not handle well or are not prepared to take action.

We do less of God's work if we do everything by ourselves. With you alone as the principal of your businesses, it is like wanting to fence your place but throwing away the pliers. In the partnership, you can lose your authority but not the ability to make decisions. Having a resourceful and dedicated team is not only an important asset for your business, it is more secure. It's no crime to invest in human management or placement consultancies. Seek out the best institutions for the provision of staff. It's okay to pay more for quality than to waste your time nurturing incompetents. Work on developing the best strategy to retain your most competent staff. Banks, phone companies, and most other businesses internally promote their most experienced or well-educated staff to learn from them. The education of the team is my priority, which is essential for the growth of the business.

Taking Calculated Risks

Calculated risk requires the qualifications of making a good judgment, basing the decision on good research, and avoiding being impulsive. It is not easy to build up taxable income when you don't venture to take risks. Many of the poor continue to be poor because they become too cautious. Calculated risks were what took place in the market. The women had access to market information that there were books available, and they knew how to use it to their advantage. Trying what you never tried in the past should never be allowed in business; that is why statistics will be very important in new discoveries. The best time to borrow money is when it is not needed. The best time to take risks is when you are comfortable and when the outcome of present actions will not be to the peril of yourself or any other person, according to Peter.

"How did the books spread in the market?" George asked the people selling his books. "The women will collect the twenty or thirty books we have in the morning, they will all read some, and then pass it around, and by the time it gets back to the owner, we can sell up to twenty copies." A smiling 60-year-old lady answered.

George moved to the synagogue in Ikorodu, but he did not forget about his friends. He visited them occasionally. Once, when George visited Ikorodu, he discovered that the books that he sold were now being sold in commercial quantities in the Ikorodu market. He discovered that ten of his initial twenty books were now selling well. The knowledge of books led to other forms of knowledge, like tips on how to dress, the kind of clothes women were wearing, how to join in a conversation with elders, and the like. George smiled in satisfaction as he continued to deliver books.

CHAPTER 32

Conclusion

Most small business people who make their first million fail largely because they are not willing to do something very basic – to follow the steps recommended here. They are asking not to embark on a quest for a new mountain of strategies and approaches they can implement, but to focus that brilliance on the right mountain, should it exist within the scope of their plans or set new plans should they require paths that are more strategic. After all, the acquisition of the first million dollars in investable capital is Mountain #1 in all of its designs. If you're not there yet, focus on getting there. After you get there, I can tell you there's another mountain that dwarfs the first. But let's get Don Johnson's pied-à-terre in Montecito Golf Club before we start focusing on a home in Barbados.

It's all very simple, isn't it? It's really not brain surgery. None of us is working at a level requiring that kind of genius. These are very basic steps. But very specific steps. There's specificity in every concept. There's also the "luck" factor – meet the right person, connect with the right investor, or get the right opportunity. But in the end, unless you are prepared, these situations will not be successful for you. Desperation leads to recklessness which often creates opportunity only to end in abject failure that becomes career crushing. By providing principles and practical tips that allow for some good aggressive good judgment, we are prescribing hope and success, not desperation and luck.